WRITE COMPELLING PLOTS
WRITE THIS WAY BOOK 4

AMANDA APTHORPE

Copyright (C) 2022 Amanda Apthorpe

Layout design and Copyright (C) 2022 by Next Chapter

Published 2022 by Next Chapter

Cover art by CoverMint

All rights reserved. No part of this book may be reproduced or transmitted in any form or by any means, electronic or mechanical, including photocopying, recording, or by any information storage and retrieval system, without the author's permission.

All internal images: Bing Creative Commons Archive

INTRODUCTION

Dear Writer

Children are great inventors of stories – all that wonderful free-wheeling, imagination and adventure.

Our family home was located on a very busy road, so my adventures were confined to the mind and were seldom acted out physically. Compare that to my partner who, between you and me, had perhaps too much physical freedom as a child to act out his imaginings, sometimes landing him in hospital.

On hearing his tales of adventures, I envied that freedom, but I came to appreciate that the life behind my young forehead was vivid and marvellous. I went through a stage when I wanted to be a 'tomboy' (I blame George in the *Famous Five* series), but the best I could do was to climb out of my bedroom window at ground level and into the backyard. Once there, I'd enact some type of tomboyish behaviour, climb back in through the window. Adventure done.

Later, I became obsessed with horses and imagined myself entering gymkhanas (usually held in the US or UK even though I live in Melbourne, Australia. Again, I blame the

INTRODUCTION

books I was reading!). My mother held a great fear of horses, which transferred itself to me, and so my contact with a real horse was very, very limited. When the central character in my favourite book fell from a horse and broke her arm, I went out in sympathy. I hid a makeshift bandage and sling in my school bag and slipped them on as I approached school. My story came undone when a family friend asked me what I had done. Knowing that our families were very likely to socialise at the weekend, I unravelled the sling and bandage and pointed to a freckle the size of a pin prick. As she contorted with laughter, I decided that I needed to keep my fertile imaginings to myself. That was, until much later, I began to write them down, to form worlds and people and scenarios. I could live in the world of my stories after all.

Can you relate to any of this? I suspect that, if you're drawn to writing, you have a vivid imagination.

We are enthralled by stories – the real and the fictional – tales told around campfires, acted on stage, written down, filmed, painted, danced and sung. Why? Because we want to be entertained, to be inspired, to escape, to enter virtual worlds, to understand and to relate to others like and unlike ourselves.

It's said that there are only seven storylines. While that might be true, those seven have generated an incredible number of readable, viewable, listenable, playable stories because – and this is the significant point that I want you to remember – the creators have told them from their own perspectives, their own point of difference.

If you have read or listened to **'Vol 2: Finding Your Writer's Voice'**, you'll be familiar with the following exercise. In that volume, the intention is to identify what has contributed, and is still contributing, to your perspective or 'take' on life and thus to understand how this has shaped your very individual writing voice. In this volume, you're going to

INTRODUCTION

mine that gold to construct, shape and enrich the showing and telling of your story.

I've provided an abbreviated version of that exercise here that asks questions for you to ponder. Take your time, but if any of the questions prompt unsettling or upsetting thoughts, move on gently.

WRITING EXERCISE 1

Pause, Think and Write after each of the questions.

1. Are you literary, conversational, or colloquial in the way you write?

Literary writing is precise and focuses on details. While it is a wonderful form of writing, I suggest that you don't force this style if you're not comfortable with it as it can lose a lot of its energy. If it's not how you think and write, the reader will pick up on that.

Conversational, or perhaps even colloquial, is your most 'natural' way of talking. Think of how you might tell a story to a friend. Because it is your most natural voice, you would relate a story with energy and ease, but there is often assumed knowledge between you and the listener. The problem with writing in this voice can be that the assumed knowledge is lost in translation, and you don't have the benefit of your facial expressions and gesticulations to convey some of the messages to the reader. Keep this in mind if you write in this voice.

What's your most natural way of writing?

2. Are you well read, or not well read?

It's important that you answer this honestly. There's no right or wrong answer; no answer better than another. In **'Volume 2: Finding Your Writer's Voice'**, I relate the story of how the supervisor for my PhD, Professor Peter Steele SJ, endorsed

INTRODUCTION

my own experience. When I confessed that I had not read the weighty tomes of literature that he often referred to because of the interruption to my own education, his response was a very gentle, 'And in that, Amanda, you are lucky.' To this day, I am still grateful to that simple comment that reassured me that my own path was significant in developing my writing voice.

3. How have the following shaped your view of life? Take your time here.

- **Your upbringing (parents/guardians/siblings/only child)**
- **Your education – good, bad or indifferent**
- **What you've read**

How has reading shaped your life? Can you remember a particular book that got you through a bad time? Or changed/influenced your view of life? Or set you on the writing path?

- **A mentor in your life**

Has there been someone you have admired who has guided you in some way? If so, what have you taken from this relationship?

4. Here's a big one:

- **Your life experience - good and bad**

Take care here. If you'd rather not revisit bad experiences, please don't; it's your call. But if comfort can be had, know that they contribute to your point of difference, and that's what we're looking for.

INTRODUCTION

Are there other factors that have contributed to your perspective?

Consider your responses to these and what have shaped you. Take a moment to read and think about your responses.

In my writing classes, and in these volumes of the *Write This Way* series, I introduce 'spontaneous' writing exercises with just a few words, the idea being that students/readers/listeners continue the words in any way they like for ten minutes. Although I haven't read or heard all of the responses to these exercises, I know that no two responses will be the same, despite the common introductory words.

What would your response to the lead-in words be? Try it now. Continue the following words for 5 minutes in any way you like:

'Shards of glass…'

Pause, Think and Write (5 minutes)

Remember, that what makes you – you, is significant for the way that you write. Hold on to this as we move forward.

Ready? **Let's go!**

PART ONE

PLOT AND STORY

Plot is no more than footprints left in the snow after your characters have run by on their way to incredible destinations.

Ray Bradbury, *Zen in the Art of Writing*

In **Writing Exercise 1**, you exercised your writer's voice. Do you think anyone else who continued those words would have written the same as you? Same genre perhaps, same tone perhaps, but not the same as you. **You are unique**. That said, no matter what the genre, the tone, the style, or the content and meaning of a story, it will relate to the human condition in some way. Even if you are creating a world unlike our own, for example in fantasy and science fiction, in order for a human reader to understand it, it needs to be relatable or believable in some way.

Some examples of human desires are for love, money, power, revenge, survival, glory and self-awareness. These are played out in stories of: overcoming a 'monster' (internal or external); a quest; voyage and return; rags to riches or riches to rages; comedy; tragedy; and rebirth. This means that we can take our cues from what's going on around us, and, no matter what genre you're writing, we can then embellish, create new worlds and scenarios in which to position our characters.

WRITING EXERCISE 2

Think of two very different stories (ideally different genres) that you have enjoyed. Can you identify any of these themes in each of them?

As a result of his work in comparative mythology and the theory of the monomyth (one myth – all mythic narratives are variations of a single great story), Joseph Campbell coined the term 'the Hero's Journey'. The template of this journey, which, in its most basic form maps the stages of a hero who goes on an adventure to gain a 'treasure', faces obstacles and a crisis, succeeds and brings the treasure home, is one that is recognised in many great myths, literature and films (think *Star Wars!*).

Some writers become a little deflated when they recognise that their story may have been told before. Okay, the storyline might match one or more of the above, but remember, it's the author's point of difference that turns it into something original, and this is an important point to remember as we move along in this section – **it's the conflicts that arise that make a story interesting.**

Before we immerse into conflict (I know, I know … sounds awful doesn't it!), let's distinguish between the terms: 'story' and 'plot'.

STORY

If someone asked you to give an overview of what your fictional piece is about, you'd tell them the STORY – the entirety of what happens to your characters who inhabit the world you have created. The who, the what and the where. Put simply, story is a series of events recorded in their chronological order.

PLOT

Now if that same person asked you more – the why, or how, or when (sounds like they might be invested in it, doesn't it), and you told them the series of events that were necessary for that story to unfold, and how the story is delivered, then you are telling them the PLOT. Put simply, a plot is a series of events deliberately arranged to reveal their dramatic, thematic, and emotional significance.

E.M. Forster put it like this: *The king died then the queen died. Story. The king died then the queen died of grief. Plot.*

WRITING EXERCISE 3

Return to one of the stories you chose in **Writing Exercise 2** above and complete the following, summarising the story in one or two sentences:

'This is a story about…'

Pause, Think and Write (1 minute)

Now think about the events that were necessary to the unfolding of that story

Pause, Think and Write (3 minutes)

Remember this exercise **Writing Exercise 3**, as I'll refer to it a number of times.

WRITING EXERCISE 4

Let's get back to you. What story do you want to write, or are you currently writing? What do you want to say? Write this down.

Pause, Think and Write (1 minute)

Whose story will you be showing and telling, that is, who is your protagonist?

In **Volume 3**, writers are encouraged to determine the desire of the central character. This is fundamental for determining the conflict that will be so important to the plot.

If you know what your central character wants, record it now. If you don't yet have a protagonist, identify what the central character wants in the story you chose in **Writing Exercise 3**. (Some to choose from are love, money, power, revenge, survival, glory and self-awareness, peace, forgiveness.)

In either case (your own protagonist, or from the story in Writing Exercise 3), how will, or how did this desire play out in the story?

WRITING EXERCISE 5

Now answer the following:

1. Why does the character want this?
2. Who or what is stopping them from getting what they want?

Pause, Think and Write (3 minutes)

THE CONFLICT

If you've read **Volume 3** of this series, you'll be familiar with the following exercise, but this time, we're going to dive deeper.

WRITING EXERCISE 6

For this exercise, I want you to think of a job, vocation, or interest that really appeals to you, that is, something that if you had the time, or had your time again, you'd want to do.

For me, this has generated the following ideal professions: librarian, research scientist, quantum physicist, naturopath, medical doctor in ER, an archaeologist, an historian who seeks out old manuscripts... Whew!

Of course, I can explore any of these interests in my novels, for example, Athena Nevis in *Whispers in the Wiring* is a neurologist, Dana Cavanagh in *A Single Breath* is an obstetrician, Cara Middleton in *Quantum Entanglement* is a quantum physicist with more than an interest in homeopathy.

Your turn but choose only one.

Now, write down a list of all the good things about that job/interest. Should be easy, right?

Pause, Think and Write (2 minutes)

Okay, now I want you to think about one challenge or conflict in that job/interest. No job or interest is perfect, so think it through.

Record it now.

Pause, Think and Write (1 minute)

We're not done yet. Now, focus on that challenge/conflict and map out a rough storyline. Invent some characters to play out the conflict, give them names. You're not writing scenes here; you're just mapping out the plot of a potential story with challenge/conflict involved.

Pause, Think and Write (3 minutes)

Did you come up with anything interesting?

If I'd ask you to map out a rough storyline based on one of the good things about that job/interest, it would be pleasant reading. But it might not be very *interesting* reading. That's because conflict or challenge provides the impetus for telling this story and it is what drives plot.

Think of it like this: **You're writing your central character's story for a reason. You've stepped into their life and picked it up at a particular point for a reason.** What is the reason? Does it relate to what they want? Does it relate to a conflict or challenge in getting what they want?

WRITING EXERCISE 7

Complete the following for your central character, or for the protagonist of the story you selected in Writing Exercise 3:

'The reader meets this character at this time of their life because…'

Pause, Think and Write (2 minutes)

STRUCTURE

WRITING EXERCISE 8

For the following exercise, record all the scenes that you have already written, or you envisage will appear in your story. If you're not there yet, you can use the story from **Writing Exercise 3**, or another one.

Here's what to do:

List these scenes in the order in which you think they will appear/or have appeared in the story. Your list doesn't need details, just words, phrases that make sense to you, for example:

1. When Harry met Sally
2. That conversation between Sally and her mother
3. The accident
4. …

Take your time with this. Try to come up with as many as possible.

Pause, Think and Write (7 minutes)

Lock this one in as I will be referring to **Writing Exercise 8** later.

. . .

Now put that aside for the moment as we meet the famous narrative arc.

If you do a search, you'll find a few representations of the narrative arc. For those who have the audio version of this book, type in 'Narrative arc' and search for one that represents the following: Exposition, Inciting Incident, Rising Action (perhaps represented as a wavy line), Climax, Denouement, and End.

Pause here if you need to locate this in a search.

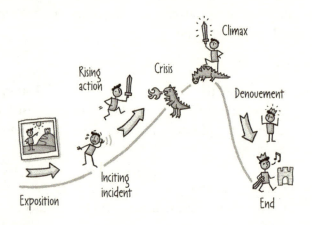

Exposition

For the reader to make any sense of what follows in a story, the exposition provides background information, or sets the scene – the setting, the introduction to a character… for the unfolding of the story. The first chapter, or few paragraphs, if not the first few lines of the opening are important to grip the reader right there and then and provide them with enough information to want to keep reading.

When we commence writing a story, the exposition can be rather messy or overdone. This is because we might be just informing ourselves of the setting, the background, and we are starting to meet our central character. Don't be too worried about this. However, when you get to the end of the draft and you know the whole story and who the main players are, then you can return to this section and rework it.

Many writers, myself included, do this. Knowing the whole story, knowing more about the characters and their motivations, enables the writer to enrich this important section.

Inciting Incident

You have stepped into or will step into the lives of your characters at this stage for a reason. Why now? What did you write for **Writing Exercise 7**? Your central character wants something, and you determined this above (and in **'Volume 3: Write Great Characters'** if you have read/listened to it).

Your central character could just keep wanting something and ultimately, not do anything, but that's not interesting. Something is holding them back; they are confined – mentally or physically – but they break free of this restriction and are propelled on a journey. Breaking free doesn't need to be a brave, conscious act by the way. It might be that their partner has left them, and they have an 'aha' moment that things need to change; it might be that they are reluctantly compelled to act for the sake of themselves, or others.

Whatever the reason, something has happened – internally, externally, or both – that incites action. This is the **INCITING INCIDENT**, and it should occur early in the story. Sometimes, this has occurred before the opening of the story.

WRITING EXERCISE 9

What is the inciting incident in your story? If you don't know yet, what propelled the central character on their journey in the story you selected in Writing Exercise 3?

Pause, Think and Write (3 minutes)

Let's continue:

Rising Action

In your capacity as a generous writer, a benefactor for your central character, you could just give them what they want straight away, couldn't you? Imagine you did this. I think you can get the picture that this would be very, very boring. Imagine if Homer had allowed Odysseus to simply return to Ithaca after the Trojan War. Nice for Odysseus, but we would have missed all that very exciting, nail-biting stuff on the way.

In the hero's journey template that we met earlier, the central character meets 'ogres' and 'assistants' on their journey, and they face a road of trials where good and bad things happen.

If this just kept going, it could become very tiring reading after a while. The momentum is building, that's why it's the rising action, and it's building to a crisis - something is about to go very, very wrong. It's often here that we find a significant **twist** in the story.

WRITING EXERCISE 10

Who/what are the helpers (assistants), and who/what are the obstacles, dangers (ogres) on your central character's journey? If you don't know this yet, who were the ogres and assistants for the character in **Writing Exercise 3**?

Note: these don't have to be other people, but could be, for example, an aspect of themselves, another animal, nature…

Do you know yet what the crisis might be? Can you identify it in **Writing Exercise 3**?

Pause, Think and Write (3 minutes)

Climax

Note the shape of the narrative arc in this book or resulting from your search. See how at least two-thirds of the story leads to the climactic moment?

Following on from the crisis discussed above, in the classic template the climax is the 'dragon-slaying moment', the point of highest tension and drama, and the central character is face-to-face with their fear, the potential loss of what they want or need. In other storylines, for example humour, this would still be a pivotal moment.

It's very important that this section is SHOWN and not TOLD (see more on this in **Part 2**). The reader, and you as the writer, need to experience this section alongside the central character.

WRITING EXERCISE 11

Do you know what this moment will be in your story? Can you identify the dragon-slaying, climactic moment in the story chosen for **Writing Exercise 3**?

Pause, Think and Write (3 minutes)

Denouement

Following the climax in our narrative arc, things start to drop off quickly, though the length of this section will vary depending on the number of characters and subplots.

In this final part of the story, the threads of the plot are woven together. While some see this as the resolution point in the story, this could have happened in the climactic scene, where the central character solved the problem. If so, then the denouement is better understood as what happens after that scene. Sometimes this is set immediately after the climax in the timeline of the story; other times, this could be a day, week, or years later.

End

Though still part of the denouement, the ending of the story needs discussion. In a classic template, the central character gains what they want and returns from the journey. Odysseus does return to Ithaca; Wonder Woman defeats the enemy. But the ending doesn't have to be successful or happy.

What your main character wants and what they need might be two different things. For example, perhaps your character wants revenge, but what they need is compassion. Are you character's wants and needs different?

Consider the following scenarios for the ending of your story where what want and need are not the same thing:

1. The protagonist gets what they want and what they need.
2. The protagonist gets what they want, but not what they need.
3. The protagonist gets what they need, but not what they want.
4. The protagonist gets neither.

No matter what the outcome, **your central character should be different in some way to when the reader met them in the exposition**. Even if the ending is 4 above, (gets neither), if they're the same as at the start, this is unsatisfying. Instead, this character might not get what they want or need, but they've acknowledged something – about themselves or life, or others, or perhaps it is that the reader who comes to understand them better. They might go on, or die, but they are not the same as when the reader met them.

WRITING EXERCISE 12

Do you know the outcome of your story, or can you identify the outcome from one of the four scenarios above in the story you chose for **Writing Exercise 3**?

Pause, Think and Write (3 minutes)

Go back to the list of scenes/events recorded in **Writing Exercise 8** for your own, or for another person's story.

Can you roughly trace a narrative arc for this story? Don't worry if it's too early for this. Revisit these exercises to see how you're tracking in plotting your story at a later time.

Bone or Cartilage?

Rather a random question, you might be thinking, but stay with me. Here's another:

What works better for a story – a tightly constructed plot, so that the writer knows from the beginning what's going to happen? (I call this a bony skeleton),

or

a more flexible plot that leaves room for changes to occur on the way? That is, the writer allows the characters a bit more freedom to direct the plot. (I call this a cartilaginous skeleton.)

The answer is … neither is the better. There are many, brilliant and successful writers who create wonderful stories with a fixed, bony plotline. This might be your preferred method. The advantage of this method is that the story stays on track, doesn't waver from the themes established by the author and, perhaps, is straightforward to write. The potential disadvantage – and in the hands of a skilled writer who knows their characters well before they write, this isn't an issue – is that flexibility can be lost as the characters develop throughout the novel.

There are other writers, myself included, who have a good idea of the plotline, but allow things to develop as they write, that is the skeleton is made of cartilage and is more flexible. The advantage of this method is that, as the characters reveal themselves (often to the author too), they 'make their own decisions'. If this sounds crazy, yes, you'd be correct. I discuss this most wonderful aspect of writing great characters in

Volume 3. To reiterate, for me the most thrilling aspect of writing stories, particularly in the long form of a novel, is when my central character 'turns to me' when I am in a scene of a bonier construction and they 'say', "No, I wouldn't do that. You'll have to change this scene." I love this! And I hope that you come to know that experience for yourself. Please note that my cartilaginous structure is still a skeleton. Yes, there might be more room to move, but I still know what the main themes of my story are, what the challenge/conflict my protagonist is enduring, and I have a good, but not fixed idea of how it will end. The disadvantage with this method, is that giving characters too much free movement can result in a mess if not handled carefully.

WRITING EXERCISE 13

Return to **Writing Exercise 8**, where you wrote down a list of the scenes/events in your story, or the story of Writing Exercise 3.

Now, scrutinise the order of that list. Consider shuffling one or more scenes around. For example, could the ending be hinted in the first scene (but not a spoiler). You can still do this even if it's someone else's work.

If there's no room to move, don't worry, the order of scenes might well be perfect as it is, but do play with it to see if you can generate fresh ideas.

Take your time with this.

Pause, Think and Write (5-10 minutes)

PITCHES

You might be familiar with the Pitch. Some publishers will open their doors for electronic submissions of unsolicited manuscripts and require that you pitch your concept (basically, convince them it's a riveting tale). You might have met this with other publications, for example, online magazines or sites that want you to pitch your short story idea.

Why is it here, you ask? After all, you might not have started your story yet. I'll get to why, but for the time being, go along with me.

In the following exercise, you will be pitching your story idea or, if you don't know your story yet, you can use the one you selected for **Writing Exercise 3**.

You must use present tense and make it as 'punchy' as you can (for example, by using strong verbs. If you've forgotten what these are, see **Part 3**)

Let's go.

WRITING EXERCISE 14

Pitch 1: What is the genre of this story (e.g., fantasy, historical romance…), and what is it about? (No more than 35 words)

Pause, Think and Write (5 minutes)

Pitch 2: Provide more detail about this story. Include the central character's name, include significant subplots where relevant. (No more than 130 words). (Think of the blurb on the back of a book, or on the landing page of an e-book.)

Remember to keep it in present tense, and to use strong language.

Pause, Think and Write (7 minutes)

Okay, you're not ready to send this off to a publisher yet, and if you struggled to do this exercise, join the club. It can be difficult to view our stories objectively and to 'talk it up'. For those of you who chose someone else's story, the exercise was probably easier for you.

I recommend that when you are writing your story, at a couple of points along the way, stop and revisit these exercises. Write these pitches again to keep you on track.

At the very least, I suggest you do the following:

Write down, using the fewest words possible, what your story is about (What did you write for **Writing Exercise 4**?). Think about why you chose to write this story, what theme/s are you exploring? If it's someone else's work, do the same.

WRITING EXERCISE 15

Continue the following: 'This is a story about...' Keep it brief!

Pause, Think and Write (1 minute)

INTERNAL STRUCTURE

Before we discuss internal structure, let's recap Point of View, discussed in Volume 3, because this might have significance for the internal structure of your story.

THE DIFFERENT POINTS VIEW

1. First person

This is the narrator of the story (a character rather than the author) and the relevant pronoun is 'I' 'we' 'me' 'my' 'our'. (In non-fiction such as autobiography, this would be the author.)

This point of view:

- has immediacy and vibrancy
- has intimacy and first-hand emotions, that is, the reader is in the heart and mind of this character

- the character telling the story can be removed from the main character (for example, Nick Caraway in *The Great Gatsby* or even one of your minor characters or extras)
- can create distance, for example, an older person reflecting on earlier life
- can be limiting in terms of what the narrator knows as the story is filtered through their consciousness. There is potential for the reader to become tired of the one perspective
- the entire story is spent with this character and with their internal monologue and external
- this character must be in every scene

Things to consider:

- you need to establish this narrator's authority for telling the story, for example, was the narrator there; how do they know what is happening; are they telling the truth?
- does the narrator have an 'axe to grind'? Is their version of the story reliable?
- if the whole story is told from their perspective, you need to build up a picture of this narrator through what they think, say, or from other characters' reactions to them, for example, in dialogue

2. Second person

This is the person being spoken to (another character, or perhaps the reader), and the relevant pronoun is 'You'.

This point of view:

- is the least used though there are several accomplished works written in this point of view

- more often used in poetry
- can sound like bullying, or finger pointing and can be unsettling to the reader
- could be a refreshing experiment. It's always good to break out of comfort zones

3. Third person

This is the person being spoken about (another character or characters) and the relevant pronouns are 'She' 'He' 'They' and other variations. This point of view is favoured by many writers. There are 3 main types of third person point of view:

- **third person subjective or limited**

This is most like first person and has all the advantages and disadvantages. The story is viewed through the character's perspective, but is written in the third person i.e., 'she/he/they'... rather than 'I' or 'we'.

This point of view:

- can have intimacy of first person and its limitations
- limited to how much the character knows
- **third person objective**

In this version of third person, the reader is viewing all characters from an objective position, and thus does not have access to their thoughts or emotions unless expressed in some other way, such as in dialogue. The 'helicopter' point of view provides an even more objective view, looking down on the character/s (from above).

This point of view:

- may have a lot of telling. Some of this might/will be necessary
- is not inside the head/heart of the character
- can be the least interesting
- **third person omniscient or authorial**

This is the god-like narrator (omniscient), or rather the author as narrator (authorial) who knows everything and is equally in the heads of all main characters.

This point of view:

- has greatest flexibility
- the narrator can go anywhere, do anything, know everything
- can break time down i.e., not limited to chronological or linear time, but can have an overall view of past/present/future
- can discuss things that characters don't know about (e.g., historical, social, political climates)
- can become intrusive
- temptation to tell rather than show everything.

Mixing points of view

It is possible to have more than one perspective in a story, for example, the protagonist's perspective and the antagonist's perspective. These might be written in first person for one, but second or third person for the other, or both in the same person.

Which point of view (or combinations) are you using? How much does your character(s) know? How much do you, the narrator know?

Can you identify the point of view in the story you selected in **Writing Exercise 3**?

Scan a few other stories – short stories or novels – and see if you can identify which point/s of view they are told from. If more than one, how does the author handle that?

It's advisable to create separate chapters or sections for each character's perspective to avoid confusion. This is particularly important if both characters' perspectives are in first person or third person subjective. Third person authorial/omniscient can enable different perspectives in the one scene.

TENSE

What tense are you writing your story in?

The most common tense choices are **simple present** and **simple past**, with simple past being the most common.

In **PART 3** of this volume, I'll provide more information on tense, but for now, let's just have a refresher of basic grammar.

Consider the following:

Jay **asked** her what she **meant**, but she **shook** her head and **walked** away.

The bolded words above are verbs and are written in the **simple past tense**, that is, having already occurred.

Jay **asks** her what she **means**, but she **shakes** her head and **walks** away.

In this sentence, the bolded verbs are in the **simple present tense**, that is, occurring now.

Be careful of mixing tenses in your story. For example:

Jay **asked** her what she **means**, but she **shook** her head and **walks** away.

Be particularly alert for these shifts if you're writing in the present tense, as it seems to be easier for some writers to slip into the past tense accidently than it is the other way around.

So, you might ask, does this mean you must stay with the same tense all the way through? Not necessarily. I discuss change of tense when writing, for example, a recollection/memory event in **PART 3**. In terms of structure here, if there is a need to change tense because, say, one character is written in present tense and another in past tense, then you will need to separate these into sections and/or chapters.

SCENE TRANSITIONS

Have you ever wondered how to move scenes in time, place, or perspective? For example, Jack is at home and takes his dog, Toto, to the shop to buy some milk. Do you need to include the actual walk, or can he just be at the shop?

The answer to this will depend on the significance of events. For example, if something important happens on the walk, or you want Jack (and the reader) to experience his neighbourhood sensually, then yes, you would include the walk. But if the walk has no significance, you can cut to the next scene.

Let's get back to Jack to see these as examples in action:

> 'Oh no, the milk's off.' Jack grimaced as he tipped the rancid milk into the sink. 'Come on, Toto, let's go for a

walk,' he called over his shoulder, at the same time throwing the carton into the recycling bin, then pulling the dog leash from the hook.

Toto pushed the wire door open with his nose and rushed down the stairs, the leash trailing between his legs.

The sun was just clipping the tops of the trees in the east as they made their way…

In this example, there are very small scene shifts. Notice that we don't see Jack put the leash on Toto, nor do we follow them down the stairs and open a gate.

Now look at this example:

'Oh no, the milk's off.' Jack grimaced as he tipped the rancid milk into the sink. 'Come on, Toto, let's go for a walk,' he called over his shoulder, at the same time throwing the carton into the recycling bin, then pulling the dog leash from the hook.

Outside the shop, Jack tied Toto to the bin post and entered…

The use of telling 'Outside the shop' is necessary to position Jack and Toto in this shift of time and place. Keep this sort of telling brief.

And this example:

'Oh no, the milk's off.' Jack grimaced as he tipped the rancid milk into the sink. 'Come on, Toto, let's go for a walk,' he called over his shoulder, at the same time throwing the carton into the recycling bin then pulling the dog leash from the hook.

Two weeks later, Jack found himself standing outside the shop dressed in his best suit. Though Toto had objected to his imminent departure from home without him, and had looked at the lead longingly, Jack had been adamant he wasn't coming this time.

The bell above the shop's door pinged as Marlowe came out to great him…

In this example, the time-shift between events is much longer. Though different publishing houses may have different styles, the larger space (and sometimes the inclusion of an asterisk, or other scene break convention), indicates scene transition. Note, too, the inclusion of brief telling words 'Two weeks later' to signal this to the reader. In a longer work, for example a novel, 'Two weeks later' might be the opening line of a new chapter.

Scene transitions can also occur when there is a shift of point of view. For example,

The bell above the shop's door pinged as Marlowe came out to greet him. She was wearing an emerald-green dress that matched her eyes and for a moment Jack was lost for words. Did he stagger? Surely not, he thought with horror.

Marlowe sized up the man in front of her and noticed how he took a small step back as she approached him.

In this example, the use of extra space, or not, will depend on the point of view that you are using.

If the story is told in third person subjective from Jack's and from Marlowe's point of view, then the shift between them in the above piece needs to be clearly marked. It's not advisable to do this too often (if at all) but is better to have each person's point of view clearly separated into distinct sections or chapters.

If the story is told in the third person authorial/omniscient, then this weaving between points of view might be more common, and thus can be paragraphed regularly. Nevertheless, this must be handled carefully to avoid confusion.

PART TWO

DESCRIPTION

about cliches. Avoid them like the plague.

Khaled Hosseini, *The Kite Runner*

We write to tell stories; we write to fulfil a need in us; we write for pleasure…

Can you relate to any of these? Why do you write?

There's such a wonderful feeling when you're in a flow moment (albeit, in my case at least, these moments can be the exception rather than the rule). When in these moments, we can feel as though we're tapping into something deeply and, if we have readers, we hope that they will feel it too. But will they?

It's a curious thing that we have thoughts and images in our mind, and then we rely on transcribing them to the page using strange symbols (alphabet and punctuation marks) and utilise grammatical constructions. As we record these images and thoughts on the page, we might be very satisfied that we have captured the essence of them. And perhaps we have, for ourselves. But has it translated effectively for the reader? Would a reader see, understand the images and thoughts we have recorded as we see and understand them?

As well as learning, understanding and applying grammatical constructions, and honing the craft of writing, we should keep the reader in mind as we write. In many of the writing exercises, in this and in other volumes of this series, you are free to write what you like. In the classes I teach, these are 'spontaneous writing' exercises, and the objective is to write without limitations. While I offer students to share their writing with the class if they want to, it's voluntary. Usually, writing this way can be hard to get going at first, but then becomes easy, and the writing flows. I see them struggle at the beginning to pick up momentum, then see how they become absorbed, their writing rate increases, and they are almost reluctant to stop.

In a different exercise, I tell them before they begin to write that they will be sharing this with a partner and that they will need to keep that reader in mind; they need to 'convince' their partner of what they're writing about. What I see is that most struggle to get going, they go back over what they've just written and cross it out and, in general, they express that the exercise is not as enjoyable as the spontaneous exercises.

Aside from lack of confidence that haunts most writers, knowing they will be sharing this writing piece with others causes them to doubt how well it will translate from their own mind to the page, then to another's mind. This is not a bad thing. When we edit what we write, what we need to keep in mind is this question: Will the reader understand or see what I do?

In previous volumes, I've mentioned that in *On Writing*, Stephen King talks of the importance of the Ideal Reader. For King, the IR is his wife, Tabitha; for me, the IR is my partner. The Ideal Reader is a person whose opinion about what you write matters to you because you trust them. If I can convince my IR, see a stirring of emotion or surprise, then I know that I've translated it well. If I see or hear a note of uncertainty or even distraction, I know I've got work to do.

Do you have an Ideal Reader? They don't have to be alive, or live close by, or even know you; they're just someone whose opinion matters (for all the right reasons) and you keep them in mind as you write, not to suffocate your own creativity, but to enhance it. If you don't want anyone to ever read your work, that's fine too, but writing with a reader in mind will help you to hone your craft.

As we go through the writing exercises in the following sections, enjoy the process for all the reasons you like to write, but think about a potential reader too.

SETTING

No matter what genre you're writing in: fantasy, contemporary, historical, sci-fi, you will create the setting/s in which the story unfolds.

Elements of setting include:

- locale – street, suburb, city, country, mountain, sea, planet...

- era – past, present or future, and perhaps more specific e.g., Korean War
- time – daytime, night time, spring, winter, Christmas...
- culture – specific religion or nationality, imposing laws and social constructions...
- weather – raining, storm, cloudy, sunny...

Can you identify the elements of setting for your own work, or the story in **Writing Exercise 3**?

Usually, these elements of setting form the background to the story, which might be appropriate for the story you're writing. However, consider the following:

1. Do you know enough about these setting elements to be convincing?
2. How will this setting and your character/s interact?

Setting and Character Interactions

Before we discuss interactions, it's important that you know the setting/s well enough to be convincing. For example, if your story is set in the Korean War, do you know enough about it? Do you need to undertake research? Or, if your story is set in a fantasy or sci-fi world, how feasible are the elements of that setting. In these worlds, setting is important in the playing out of the lives of characters. Though you can have freedom in inventing a new and unfamiliar world, it still needs to be convincing for the reader to be able to 'inhabit' it, along with the characters.

Even if your setting more often forms the background to your story, bringing it forward every now and then can add a rich dimension for your characters', for your own, and for your reader's experience.

Consider the following ways of showcasing your setting:

1. Setting as a character with a mood or attitude (personification)

We often use terms such as 'miserable weather', 'gloomy sky', 'friendly neighbourhood', the 'witching hour'. These types of expressions are so commonly used that we don't really notice that we are attributing human moods and attitudes to such elements of setting.

In these expressions, we're just attaching an adjective e.g., friendly, to the element. What if we played on this mood/attitude even more, for example,

The weather coated her in its misery.

Dark clouds colluded to form deep furrows in the forehead of the sky.

The neighbourhood wrapped them in its welcoming arms.

The hour cast its dark spell as I whimpered beneath the blanket.

There is the implication that the character or narrator has an attitude to the setting, that is, they are in harmony, or in conflict with it. Let's explore how to build on this interaction between character and setting.

2. Setting as experienced through the senses

We experience the world through our five senses (some might say, six): sight, hearing, taste, feel and smell (and insight). Although all these senses are powerful, generally we tend to be more aware of sight and hearing, and this can be particularly true when we're describing our characters' experience of their world.

Allowing your characters to experience their world through the other senses (taste, touch, smell, and perhaps insight) can provide a much richer experience of setting.

For example, does the weather feel dank as it coats her in its misery?

Could the smell of ozone accompany the furrowing of clouds in the sky?

What do the 'welcoming arms' of the neighbourhood feel like, or does it taste or smell like apple pie? What does the hour's dark spell feel like, smell like?

We'll look at senses in more detail under Figurative Language.

WRITING EXERCISE 16

Apply this exercise to a character in your story, or if you don't have one yet, invent one now.

Continue the following words to bring setting into the foreground and have your character experience it through either smell, taste, or touch.

'At night, the street was…'

Pause, Think and Write (5 minutes)

As well as convincing a reader, enabling them to understand or see what we do, we want our reader to feel it too, to be moved by an emotion, a memory. I could add that we want them to be impressed by our ability with words, but the problem is, we might try just a bit too hard to do that.

Have you ever had the feeling of great pride, and even a small or large amount of 'how clever am I' when you've written a sentence, a paragraph, or a scene? If so, be wary of this. While it might be brilliant, there's also the possibility that it's too contrived, is unlike your natural writing voice and thus out of tempo, and it leaps from the page: it's too self-conscious.

You might have heard the expression 'kill your darlings', and this is what these contrived sections are – your darlings. You're proud of them, but… you might need to kill them off.

This type of self-conscious writing is different from the writing you do when you're in the zone, when you're tapping into something deep within yourself; the sort of things that might send a quiver up your spine and get you hooked on this writing thing. Know the ones I mean?

In '**Volume 2: Finding Your Writer's Voice**', I explore this deep aspect of the authentic and the dynamic you, and this is wholly relevant here as I explore the story element of description.

FIGURATIVE LANGUAGE

Figurative language 'dresses up' our descriptions by making comparisons between the concrete and the abstract via the senses.

There are several types of figurative language, but here we will focus on four: metaphor, simile, cliché and symbolism. Personification is also a type of figurative language, and we met this under Setting.

Metaphor

A metaphor provides an implied comparison between two things by using words or phrases that might be used for one of those things and applying them to the other. They are figures of speech that are not true in a literal way.

Sound confusing? Let's have a look at some examples:

1. He was a bear of a man.

In this simple metaphor, it's implied that the man is a bear. But this isn't a literal meaning; rather, it suggests that the man is large, powerful (and maybe even very hairy!).

2. In the examples under Setting, we met '**...deep furrows in the forehead of the sky.**' Again, it's implying a comparison between the gloomy look of clouds in the sky and the furrowed forehead of a gloomy human but is not meant to be understood literally.

Simile

A simile makes a comparison between two things though doesn't suggest that one thing 'is' the other. The words 'like' and 'as' are often used here to show this relationship, while maintaining some separation between the two things compared.

For example:

1. He was big, like a bear.

Unlike the example used above for metaphor, here the 'he' and the bear are distinguished from each other by the word 'like'.

2. '... deep furrows formed as though the sky had a forehead...' Here, the inclusion of 'as' distinguishes the deep furrows of clouds, and a human forehead.

Cliché

Clichés are overused similes, metaphors, sayings that have lost their impact because they are too familiar. They are so embedded in our language that we often don't know that we're using them e.g., 'actions speak louder than words'; love is blind; ignorance is bliss; you can't judge a book by its cover... However, you could have a character who speaks this way.

When such expressions were first used, they were original and enriched the text, but be wary of overused expressions and comparisons, for example, rather than describing very wrinkled skin as 'like an elephant's hide' think of something that the wrinkled skin reminds you of – the fissures in a dry creek bed; rather than describing light glinting off the sea as 'jewels' consider the movement of them, the intermittent flashes that reminds you of...?

In the picture above of the moon on the lake (if you have the audio version of this book, search for an image of the moon reflected clearly in a lake), consider the reflection as the real moon and the real moon the reflection; or the reflection as something emerging from the depths of the lake

Metaphor and simile as symbolism

Imagine that a butterfly has landed on your protagonist's arm. What does your protagonist think of it? Using simile or metaphor, how might this butterfly represent an aspect of your character's personality or life so far i.e., what could this butterfly symbolise?

While using metaphor and simile are wonderful ways of enriching your narrative, don't overuse them, otherwise it can become suffocating for the reader. A wonderful simile that someone used to describe the overuse of metaphor in an author's novel was: 'It was like being in an overly-perfumed room'. 'Less is more', though a cliché now, is still wise advice.

Invent your own metaphors and similes BUT be careful that they represent something that the reader can understand. Fortunately, we have a large repertoire of expressions that can be understood. In the exercise above, would the reader understand the symbolism of the butterfly?

In the following exercise, let your imagination flow and then ask yourself, would the reader understand this?

WRITING EXERCISE 17

Write a descriptive piece e.g., an empty restaurant, or a fictional character's bedroom. Include within the space something minute (i.e., very, very small), something oversized, and something dark.

Choose your own metaphor to describe the 'something dark'. Be adventurous and avoid clichés.

Pause, Think and Write (5 minutes)

USING THE SENSES

Using all five senses in your writing increases your chances of connecting with your readers. Too frequently, we limit our characters' reception of their world to sight and hearing. While these two might well dominate the sensual elements in the story, remember that there are another three senses that can add richness to your characters', your own, and your reader's experience.

Let's start with the most common – sight and hearing. Rather than them just providing routine information, bring them forward as though your character is experiencing something through these senses for the first time.

WRITING EXERCISE 18

Bring your character into a scene they've never been in before. It could be inside a building, in a new town or city, a first visit to a nursing home.

What do they see? Don't just tell it, but zone in to provide details of a handful of visual prompts – an oversized atrium, prominent architecture, an unkept bed.

What sounds does your character hear?

Pause, Think and Write (5 minutes)

WRITING EXERCISE 19

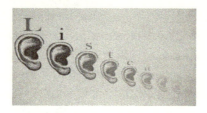

Now let's step it up.

Imagine that your character is contained in some way, for example, imprisoned in a dark room, stuck in a lift at night. Choose something relevant to your character and the genre of your story.

As their sight is limited, their hearing becomes more acute. What do they hear?

Pause, Think and Write (3 minutes)

Smell works differently for each of us. What one person might think is a bad smell, someone else might not be bothered by – or might love it.

Smell is an important sense as it brings back memories and ignites strong feelings.

As an example, when I was fourteen, our parents took us on a six-day cruise. The ship was old, but I thought it was magnificent. Most significantly, I remember the dining room (eating has always been a favourite pastime!), but it was the smell of that room rather than the food that was most memorable. This will sound unpleasant, but the odour was Freon gas used in the large refrigerators (and highly toxic I now believe). To this day, should I be walking along a busy lane in Melbourne, and I smell that refrigerator gas, I am immediately transported to that dining room and am fourteen all over again.

I'm sure you will relate to an odour or scent conjuring memory. Allow this sense to do the same for your character. A smell can be a wonderful prompt to enable backstory to be revealed.

WRITING EXERCISE 20

Record 2 odours/scents that would have significance for your character. You can draw on your own experience here.

Now, write a paragraph that introduces the smell in real time and then transports your character back into the past.

Pause, Think and Write (5 minutes)

Like all senses, touch can be painful or pleasurable – the searing pain of a burn, the comfort of a loving hand.

Sometimes, a touch is neither painful nor pleasurable, but simply forms an experience in our mind, for example something we see and know that we don't want to touch – a greasy pan, a dead animal. What repels and attracts us is subjective. For example, while I love the taste of peaches, I can't bear to touch the furry skin, and even thinking about that now prompts my teeth to clench at the thought.

Sometimes the touch itself is what is important, not what the thing being touched feels like. A character reaching out to touch another character can be extremely powerful under the right circumstances, as can the laying of a hand on a headstone.

WRITING EXERCISE 21

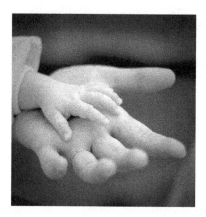

Record one touch sensation that would have significance for your character. You can draw on your own experience here.

Now, write a paragraph that introduces this element and how touching it makes your character feel.

Pause, Think and Write (5 minutes)

How do you relate to the sense of taste? Is there a taste that disturbs you? excites you? comforts you?

The sense of smell and the sense of taste are closely related. If you've ever lost your sense of taste because of a cold or other condition, you know how that affects the pleasurable experience of eating.

WRITING EXERCISE 22

What if your character has lost the sense of taste – temporarily or permanently. How would this affect them? Have them describe the taste that they miss the most.

Pause, Think and Write (5 minutes)

Show, don't just tell

You might have heard the advice to 'show not tell' in your creative fiction. Telling is stating facts and provides an overview, for example, 'Jaimie remembered how his aunt would place the Tarot cards on the table, then ask him to select one with his eyes closed.' In this scenario, telling has an important role in fiction enabling for the recounting of a memory. In addition, telling is necessary for positioning characters in time and place, for example, 'Three weeks later, Ravi was sitting at the table with his oldest friend eating pizza.'

Too much telling, on the other hand, lacks richness and does not enable the reader to experience along with the characters. What is satisfying for a reader is being able to piece things together, rather than to be just told what is happening. Look out for this in your use of adverbs. I've addressed this in Volume 3 in the section on dialogue but will restate it here. Rather than telling the reader someone is angry: 'Don't say that again,' she said angrily, show it instead by painting the picture: 'Don't say that again.' The colour had drained from her face and her jaw was thrust forward in defiance.

The act of showing is a demonstration or dramatisation of how something is done, how something happened, how something appears, or what something feels like.

Let's revisit Jaimie in real time.

'As he held the cards, he was aware of their weight, and something else – an almost imperceptible vibration. He dealt them slowly, glancing every now and then at Ravi who he could tell was holding his breath.'

In this example, rather than just relating the scene, concrete details are provided to enrich the experience. The reader senses that something is going to happen, and that Ravi is nervous.

While most of your story should be shown rather than told (especially the climax!), too much showing can be draining for the reader. Telling has its place, so remember the advice is **'Show, don't just tell.'**

Okay, hopefully, you're feeling more confident about plotting your story, enriching it using figurative language and using the senses, and determining a healthy mix of showing and telling.

In **Part 3: Editing Toolbox,** I've identified common editing issues that many of my writing students face, and perhaps you can relate to these too. We'll look at basic punctuation, grammar rules and formatting considerations that commonly arise in writing fiction with examples to demonstrate correct use.

Ready? Let's go.

PART THREE

EDITING TOOLBOX

When it comes to editing our own work, most of us struggle with one or more elements of grammar, punctuation, spelling and formatting.

Does editing your own work feel like a drag at times – the less interesting part of being a writer? Many can relate to this. But is it more to do with the attitude we bring to it rather than the process itself?

Remember that, as writers, we only have these strange symbols: letters, numerals, punctuation marks, and the formatting of these: italics, capitals, use of white space... to transcribe the idea or image in our mind onto the page, and then for it to faithfully translate into the reader's mind. Whooh! What a feat!

We can include visual images and sound of course (such as the audio version of this book, but even then, it comes down to the narrator taking their cue from the symbols in front of them); however, most of the work will be in the written word.

What is your process for editing your work? Are you a perfectionist and don't feel happy moving on to the next sentence until you've perfected the first? Do you write freely for a few thousand words and then edit it in 'batches'? Do you write straight through to the end and then edit the work from start to finish?

My own process is batching. After three thousand words of un-edited work, I start to get a bit anxious, for two reasons: In addition to this series, I write novels, and the idea of editing a whole 80,000+ words for the first time seems too daunting, and the 'danger' of leaving it that long to edit is that you can miss out on significant shifts and ideas that may have repercussions further down the line. I write from beginning to end in that order for the same reason. Some writers record scenes as they arise in their mind and piece the story together later. Many do this successfully, but I worry that if things change along the way, those scenes might not be relevant anymore. As I write freely and in hard copy (usually in a coffee shop), I make notes to myself, for example, if I know a word chosen isn't the one that I really want, but can't think of a better one at the time, I circle the word; if a sentence is not great, my margin notes can border on the mildly insulting e.g., 'That's lame, Mand', but I don't want to break the creative output that comes with writing in flow moments (accompanied by the scent of coffee beans).

Let me make it clear though, my process is my own. I know that the perfectionists amongst you must fix things as you go, or you just don't feel right about it; I know that wonderful creative output can come from just writing from start to finish (or in scenes to be pieced together later). As I emphasised in 'Volume 2: Finding Your Writer's Voice', you must develop your own patterns of writing and of editing, but as long as these are truly working for you.

Let's get back to that attitude. When we understand that editing is the crafting of those symbols to shape our work ready for successful transfer to the reader's mind, then we appreciate that editing is just as creative as the free writing process.

The following is not an intensive lesson in English grammar and punctuation. There are many excellent books available that will provide you with a 'back-to-basics' approach, or more advanced discussions. The topics included here are those that I have identified as being some of the most common editing issues that my writing students grapple with, and you might relate to these too.

I have divided **Part 3** into three sections: **Punctuation, Grammar** and **Formatting**. (For spelling issues, refer to the most authoritative dictionary in your country.)

Please note that different English-speaking countries have some variations in rules of grammar, for example, the use of the Oxford comma. In addition, publishing houses have editing styles that they prefer, for example, use of single or double quotation marks in dialogue; spelling variations; representations of numbers as word or numeral; para-graphing conventions... It is important that you check the submission guidelines before sending off your work for consideration.

Ready? Let's go!

PUNCTUATION

The most common punctuation problems arising in fiction are those in dialogue. I have already addressed these in the DIALOGUE section of 'Volume 3: Write Great Characters', but they're worth revisiting here, specifically: quotation marks, commas, end punctuation, ellipsis points and em dashes.

As I'm an Australian, I will be punctuating according to the Australian English standards; however, variations from other countries' English standards are minor.

1. Comma and full stop placement

Consider the following:

'Hey, Joe,' Laura said noticing that he was limping. 'What have you done to yourself?'

Note the placement of the first comma. This is used when addressing someone, for example: My dear friend, Dr Jones.

(In Australian spelling, the full stop is not included after titles, for example, Dr, Mr, Mrs, Ms, Mme, if the end letter of the full word is the same as that in the abbreviated version. This differs in US spelling.)

The second comma ends the sentence IF followed by an attribution/explanatory word (such as they said, she whispered, he muttered, we shouted...)

Note the difference in the following:

'Hey, Joe.' Laura noticed that he was limping. 'What have you done to yourself?'

In this example, the sentence Hey, Joe. is not followed by an attribution (such as 'said'). We know that it is Laura saying it, but the words aren't directly attributed to her. The sentence needs its appropriate end punctuation, in this case it is the full stop.

In the following example, the two sentences are combined into one, but the attribution splits it. Note the punctuation around it.

'Hey, Joe,' Laura said noticing that he was limping, 'what have you done to yourself?'

In this example, notice the inclusion of the third comma that indicates that the next section of dialogue belongs in the same sentence; the word 'what' is not capitalised.

2. The question mark and exclamation mark placement

What happens if a question or exclamation mark comes before the attribution?

'What have you done to yourself?' Laura said noticing that he was limping.

'What have you done to yourself?' Laura noticed that he was limping.

In each of these examples, with and without the attribution 'said', the question mark is sufficient to end the sentence (question).

The same is true for the exclamation mark, for example:

'Ah!' Joe said with a roll of his eyes. 'I have no idea!'

In each of the examples above, the comma, full stop, question mark or exclamation mark is INSIDE the closing quotation mark. Please check with your country's standard or publication house's style for variations.

3. Quotation marks

In the examples shown above, single quotation marks have been used for dialogue. In the Australian English standard, this is more recent advice. Double quotation marks are used for quotes within quotes, for example:

'I can't believe she said, "I never want to talk to you again", after all you've done for her.'

Despite this instruction to my students, most will still use double quotation marks for dialogue, and single for quotes within quotes. This is what they had been taught (as I had been) and it seems too hard to make the change.

"I can't believe she said, 'I never want to talk to you again', after all you've done for her."

Double quotation marks are not incorrect, and you will find that they are still used frequently, and this might be the standard in your own country. Don't forget to check the publisher's submission requirements.

The important things to remember:

1. Whatever you use for dialogue, use the opposite for the quote within a quote, and
2. Be consistent in that choice all through the work.

4. Interruptions and pauses

In dialogue, you might have one person interrupt another, or have one person hesitate or trail off something they're saying.

Let's continue with Laura and Joe:

'Hey, Joe,' Laura said noticing that he was limping. 'What have—'

'Ah! Don't ask.'

In this example, Joe interrupts Laura's question. The em dash is useful to show this as it is a visually disruptive symbol that announces something. The em dash is the longest of the dashes and there is no space between it and 'have'.

Compare this to:

'Hey, Joe,' Laura said noticing that he was limping. 'What have you...'

'Ah! You noticed,' Joe said.

In this example, there is a softer interruption, or Laura trails off in what she is saying as Joe approaches. Three ellipsis points are used here. Don't include a fourth ellipsis as a full stop.

5. Thoughts

Ever been unsure how to represent a character's thoughts? The following demonstrate three ways to do this:

1. Use quotation marks as you would for direct speech in dialogue, for example, 'He's not looking very happy,' Laura thought.
2. Don't use quotation marks, for example, He's not look very happy, Laura thought.
3. Use italics to show distinction of thoughts from direct speech, for example, *He's not looking very happy*. In this case, you don't need the attribution 'Laura thought'.

Whichever you choose, use this **consistently** throughout the work.

General punctuation rules

In this section, I've hand-picked several punctuation symbols that can cause other problems relevant in writing fiction.

1. Comma

Above we met the use of the comma in dialogue in relation to the attribution, and also when using direct address. The more common use of the comma is to create a pause within a sentence. However, the positioning of a pause is not random. Given that we breathe at different rates, imagine the chaos if we just planted a comma where we felt the need for a breath!

Use a comma to join two main clauses together using a coordinating conjunction

Have I lost you? Hold on. I'll explain with a quick revision of the main clause.

A main clause makes sense on its own. It has a subject and a verb, and if we include an end punctuation (full stop, question mark or exclamation mark), we turn it into a sentence. For example:

the dog barked all night

This makes sense on its own. It has a subject 'the dog' and a verb 'barked', so I can now turn this into a sentence: The dog barked all night.

Here's another one:

the cat slept all day

This makes sense on its own. It has a subject 'the cat' and a verb 'slept', so I can now turn this into a sentence. The cat slept all day.

What if I bring these two clauses together to make one sentence? I'll need one of three things: a coordinating conjunction, a conjunctive adverb, or a semi-colon.

Here goes:

The dog barked all night, and the cat slept all day.

In this example, I have joined them with 'and', which is a coordinating conjunction. I could have used another e.g., 'but'. Check out other coordinating conjunctions in a grammar search. Note the position of the comma before the coordinating conjunction.

Alternatively, these clauses could be joined with a conjunctive adverb, or a semi-colon, for example:

The dog barked all night; however, the cat slept all day. In this example, 'however' is the conjunctive adverb joining the clauses. Note the punctuation – a semi-colon before it and a comma after it.

The dog barked all night; the cat slept all day. In this example, the two main clauses are simply joined with a semi-colon. This way of joining main clauses can be effective and can provide a particular tempo in your writing; however, the two clauses must be related to each other in context.

<u>Use a comma after introductory words, phrases or clauses</u>

Commas are required after introductory words, phrases, or clauses, for example:

Unfortunately, Max knew about his surprise party ahead of time.

In the evening, Charlie chopped wood and set the fire for the long night ahead.

Although they'd arrived, nobody wanted to be the first to go in.

There are several other uses for the comma that I won't go into here. I suggest that you consult a reliable grammar book for more information.

2. Commas, dashes and parentheses

I've grouped these three as they can serve the same function when used to separate asides/non-essential information and appositives as in the following examples:

The book, you know the one, that I gave you last month has been made into a movie.

The book—you know the one—that I gave you last month has been made into a movie.

The book (you know the one) that I gave you last month has been made into a movie.

The main sentence above is: The book that I gave you last month has been made into a movie. Note that the non-essential information, or aside you know the one can be separated from the main sentence in one of three ways.

In fiction, the more common practice is to use either commas (most common), or dashes; however, the dash is more visually disruptive than the comma. If the aside/non-essential information is dramatic, then this would be a good choice. In this example, I have used the em dash, the longest dash, and this is unspaced. Some writers prefer to use the shorter en dash and with spaces either side. Parentheses are not often used in fiction as they are more formal than the comma and em dash. Whichever you choose, ensure that you keep choice of dash and spacing consistent throughout your story. And don't forget to check publishers' submission guidelines.

(Note: the hyphen is not a dash and would be incorrectly used here.)

3. Semi-colon

We have met a function of the semi-colon above in joining two main clauses together. Before choosing this option (as compared to other alternatives above), consider the effect on the tempo of your sentence. For example,

The night was hot; the sweat trickled down my body.

Compare this to:

The night was hot, and the sweat trickled down my body. (Comma and coordinating conjunction).

OR

The night was hot; subsequently, the sweat trickled down my body. (Conjunctive adverb).

The use of the semi-colon in the first example provides a more dramatic feel that is diluted in the other two examples. I recommend that you don't overuse the semi-colon in this way; keep it for 'special effects'.

The semi-colon, like the colon, is a rather formal punctuation mark. As such, it can look out of place in dialogue, even if there are correct grammatical reasons for including it. (Consult a grammar text for other uses).

4. Apostrophe

A reminder that the apostrophe is used in fiction to show possession, or contraction/omission. For example,

My aunt's teapot was made in Japan. Singular possession

Their parents' car is old, but it still runs well. Plural possession

"I can't go 'cause I don't have anythin' to wear." In this example, the apostrophes indicate the letters missing. When writing dialogue, it is good to use contractions such as: can't, don't, I'm, you've as they can sound more natural.

Please be careful of it's and its. With the apostrophe it's means it is, without the apostrophe its shows possession e.g., the cat licked its fur.

GRAMMAR

1. The sentence

A sentence begins with a capital letter, has a subject and a verb and ends with a full stop, a question mark, or an exclamation mark. A sentence makes complete sense in itself.

The rise of text messaging is bringing about some changes to the way that some people write, such as not capitalising the first word in a sentence, not ending a sentence with the appropriate punctuation, and presenting phrases or subordinate clauses as sentences that don't make complete sense in themselves.

While these short cuts may be wholly appropriate for messaging, they don't have a place in narrative fiction, unless you are representing a character's text message as a form of dialogue.

Consider the following:

Peta vowed that she would never go there again. No matter how much she might want to. she was afraid. Of what she might do

Peta vowed that she would never go there again. is a complete sentence.

No matter how much she might want to. is a subordinate clause and doesn't make sense on its own. It relies on the context provided by the main clause.

she was afraid. Would be a sentence but requires the capitalised 'She'.

Of what she might do is also a subordinate clause and doesn't make sense on its own.

Correct version:

Peta vowed that she would never go there again no matter how much she might want to. She was afraid of what she might do.

Note: A phrase or subordinate clause can add a dramatic appeal when presented as a sentence. In the above example, it could be argued that No matter how much she might want to is represented on its own to add impact or emphasis. This can work well but be careful that it is delivering the effect you're intending, not simply highlighting poor editing skills. Similarly, an older grammatical rule was that you shouldn't start a sentence with a conjunction such as 'but' or 'and'. But sometimes, this can provide a suitable emphasis.

Sentence lengths

Varying sentence lengths can create rhythm or a tempo to your writing that can be very effective for engaging the reader.

A series of long sentences slows the reading down and can create a whimsical, languid feeling.

A series of short sentences are crucial in action or very tense scenes.

TIP: Provide a good mix of long and short sentences in your paragraphs unless aiming for the effects mentioned above.

2. The mighty verb

If there is a powerhouse in your editing toolbox, it is the verb.

A reminder: a verb is an action/doing word e.g., run, think, bake…, or a state of being/linking word e.g., am, are, was, were, will be…

When you are editing your work, consider the choices available to you, especially for the action/doing verbs. A good thesaurus is your friend here.

Compare the two sentences below:

The milk truck went quickly around the corner then stopped suddenly.

The milk truck swerved around the corner then screeched to a halt.

In the first sentence, went needed the adverb quickly, and stopped needed the adverb suddenly to provide more information.

While the reader will get the idea of what the milk truck did, it's hardly exciting.

In the second version, swerved and screeched are more effective verb choices and they don't require a modifier to provide more oomph.

Adverbs can be unnecessarily maligned. Here I am talking about the adverbs that end in 'ly' such as angrily, sweetly, quietly etc.You will read guides that tell you to remove all adverbs within your story, and, as a rule, this is good advice. But sometimes the perfectly chosen adverb can add to the strength of the verb.

Next time you're reading a novel or short story, see if you can spot any adverbs and decide whether they work, or if the sentences require stronger verbs instead.

(Did you spot the adverb in the sentence beginning with 'But' above? 'perfectly').

Subject-verb agreement

A quick recap: Remember that a subject and verb in a sentence need to agree, that is, if you have a singular subject, you need to have a singular verb. For example:

My sister are going to the party, and they is going too.

I'm sure you can spot the problem here.

My sister is singular and requires the singular verb 'is', while they are plural and requires the plural verb 'are'.

Usually, these agreements are obvious, but in some examples, they are less clear.

A herd of cows is/are in the field. What is your choice here? The correct answer is A herd of cows is in the field. This is because a herd is the simple subject, and it is singular.

There are other rules of subject-verb agreement. If this is a limitation for you, I suggest you consult a reliable grammar text.

Note: The use of the plural 'they' to represent a singular person is becoming more popular. At present, the plural form of the verb is used even if referring to a single person, e.g., Harry was invited to the party, and they are going.

Active and Passive voice of the verb

I'll make this quick as I'm sure the heading is going to tempt you to finish right here.

Generally, you should default to writing in the active form.

So, what do I mean? Consider the following:

The watch was given to me by my grandmother on my thirteenth birthday.

Okay, this might sound fine. You understand the meaning of the sentence; however, it is unnecessarily verbose. This sentence is in the passive voice and would be far simpler if reworded to be in the active form:

My grandmother gave me the watch for my thirteenth birthday.

In the sentence above, the grandmother is the do-er of the action of giving and so should go into the subject position at the start of the sentence.

There are times when the passive voice is the correct or only choice, for example when you don't know who the do-er of the action is. For example,

The body was found at the bottom of the stairs.

In this sentence the 'finder' is not known, so the passive voice is appropriate.

Or you want to bring attention to the receiver of the action. For example,

My country was attacked by the enemy during the war.

Here, the emphasis is on 'my country'. The active version would be:

The enemy attacked my country during the war.

Sometimes, writing in the passive voice (when it should, technically, be the active voice) can provide a lyrical quality. For example:

Know that you are loved.

If this was converted to the active, the do-er of loving would need to be included:

I love you.

Nice sentiment in both cases, and yes, the active is more concise, but the passive version lends a lyrical, poetic quality to the writing.

Note: Always use active voice for action scenes!

Enough said? Okay. If you want to know more, consult that grammar text!

Tense

Of all the grammatical errors I see in my students' writing, it is the shifting of tense that is the most common.

Tense provides a sense of the time of an event or action in relation to the time of speaking or writing of that event or action.

Time is broadly divided into past, present and future, but each of these have sub-categories.

Consider the following table (if you have the audio version of this book, locate in a search engine, a table or other that depicts all versions of past, present and future tenses):

PAST	PRESENT	FUTURE
Simple past: She ran	Simple present: She runs	Simple future: She will run
Past perfect: She had run	Present perfect: She has run	Future perfect She will have run
Past progressive: She was running	Present progressive: She is running	Future progressive: She will be running
Past perfect progressive: She had been running	Present perfect progressive: She has been running	Future perfect progressive: She will have been running

Are you having hysterics? Stay calm; I'm not going to talk about all of these. You can consult that grammar text at your leisure, but I do want to point out the most common errors I see.

The popular choices for writing tense are the simple past or the simple present. Here's an example of the same text in each tense:

Simple Past

When Charlie arrived home, he made a cup of tea and toast and sat down at the table in the small dining room. Flick, his cat, purred as she rubbed against his leg. 'Good girl,' he said as he lifted her to his lap.

Simple Present

When Charlie arrives home, he makes a cup of tea and toast and sits down at the table in the small dining room. Flick, his cat, purrs as she rubs against his leg. 'Good girl,' he says as he lifts her to his lap.

It is important that you maintain the tense consistently.

For example:

When Charlie arrives home, he made a cup of tea and toast and sat down at the table in the small dining room. Flick, his cat, purred as she rubs against his leg. 'Good girl,' he said as he lifts her to his lap.

Each of the verbs here are in the simple past, but the paragraph opens in the present. The tense slips from one to the other after that.

Past perfect

When you have a scene that involves flashback, memory or recounting something that has already happened, use the past perfect. This form of the tense includes the verb 'had'.

For example:

Charlie had decided that he would never go to the football again. When he arrived home, he made a cup of tea…

In this example, 'had decided' informs the reader that this decision was made earlier, before he arrived home.

Or a longer memory:

Charlie had always known that he was different to others. He'd gone to the same school as the children in his village, but he'd always felt out of place. The other students bullied him, and some boys chased him home after school.

In this example, the use of the past perfect 'he had known', 'he'd gone', 'he'd felt' keeps the reader in a more distant past. It's not necessary to maintain the past perfect all the way through a section like this. Note 'the other students bullied' 'chased', which are in the simple past.

As you can see from the table, the use of tense is more complex that just these examples. Consult a reliable grammar text for more information as needed.

3. Parallel constructions

Another consideration for maintaining tempo/rhythm in your writing, is the correct use of parallel constructions. These constructions are popular in rhetoric and in many well-known speeches. You might not be writing a speech, but parallelisms are important in maintaining the tempo of your ideas expressed in a sentence.

Consider the following:

Though it was Brahmi's birthday, she loved to cook for her friends, set up the party lights and spreading out the special birthday tablecloth.

In this sentence, Brahmi loves to do three things: to cook, to set up and spreading. While the first two are parallel, the third, 'spreading' is not. We need to rework them so that they are aligned, or parallel.

Correct version 1: Though it was Brahmi's birthday, she loved to cook for her friends, to set up the party lights and to spread out the special birthday tablecloth.

OR

Correct version 2: Though it was Brahmi's birthday, she loved cooking for her friends, setting up the party lights and spreading out the special birthday tablecloth.

In each of these correct versions, you can see that the same structure is repeated providing a rhythm to the prose; it would now be a matter of choosing which one you prefer.

4. Incorrect positioning of modifiers

Modifiers (e.g., adjectives, adverbs, phrases...) provide more information about other words.

Consider the following:

The spider scaled the wall.

It's okay, but not very interesting. Try this:

The black, hairy spider scaled the rough texture of the wall.

By providing more information about the spider and the wall, a more vivid image is created for the reader.

However, if the modifier is positioned away from the word it is modifying, it can cause confusion. For example,

Scaling the rough texture of the wall, the woman was frightened by the black, hairy spider.

In this example, the modifier is 'Scaling the rough texture of the wall'. The noun phrase it is modifying is 'the black, hairy spider', but it is positioned too far away from it. Instead, the sentence reads as though it is the woman who scaled the rough texture of the wall.

Consider this one:

Cycling up hills quickly tires muscles.

The modifier here is 'quickly', an adverb that is providing more information about...? Which verb – cycling, or tires? This would need to be reworded for clarity:

Cycling quickly up hills tires muscles.

FORMATTING

1. Paragraphing

Have you ever turned the page of a story, or on screen, and found yourself face-to-face with a whole block of text that is not paragraphed?

Your reader has a visual relationship with the page, and paragraphing is an important part of that.

However, paragraphs can't be randomly placed. Like all of the elements we've discussed in **Part 3** so far, there are rules for use. Thank goodness. If there weren't then writers could make up their own. This could work, but it's risky.

The rule for paragraphing is easiest understood by using the following acronym:

TiPToP

Create a new paragraph when there is a change in:

Ti = time

P = place

To = topic

P = perspective.

(Remember that the convention for writing dialogue is to start a new paragraph for each person speaking. That's a change in perspective.)

There are two options for formatting paragraphs: indenting OR extra spacing.

Check the publishers' submission guidelines for formatting preference.

If you have big shifts in any of the above, create scene breaks. You can do this by including an extra space and can include a bullet point or asterisk centred in the page, or you could separate it into a new chapter.

2. Other considerations

As mentioned above, the reader has a visual relationship with the page. As such, keep the following in mind:

- As a rule, use words rather than numerals in fiction e.g., a six-year-old boy, rather than a 6-year-old boy; 'in two days' time' rather than 'in 2 days' time. However, you are not incorrect if you use numerals, and this might be more appropriate in some genres.
- Limit the use of full capitalisations e.g., 'DON'T SAY THAT!' they shouted. Find more creative ways of indicating this. Perhaps onlookers stop to see what the noise is about, or the recipient has to block their ears. Full capitalisation in representation of text messages might be appropriate.
- *If you're choosing to use italics for thoughts as discussed above, be aware of how often these would appear on the page. If your character does a lot of thinking, you might consider one of the other ways of representing thoughts, as discussed above. Italics can also be more difficult to read than roman.*
- Name/nickname representations and terms of endearment.

Consider the following:

My mum picks me up because Mum and I live a long way from the school.

When referring to 'mum' (and other such names) generically, use the lower case. When using as a name, use upper case M.

For terms of endearment, e.g., darling, love, sweetheart, use the lower case:

'Yes, darling,' Mum said, 'I'll pick you up at three o'clock.'

3. Less is more

Be mindful of overwriting. There can be a temptation, especially when we are new writers, to try too hard to impress – ourselves and others. Beautiful, figurative language is great, but paring back your writing doesn't 'dumb it down'. Exquisite writing is what is contained within those words, rather than the number of them. Every word should have a role in your sentences.

If you have struggled with any of the above in your own writing, I hope that they are clearer to you now. Do remember that I have targetted those areas that I see most commonly in others' writing (and my own!), but for a more comprehensive understanding of any of these elements, consult a reliable grammar text.

While it is within our capacity to do it, editing our own work has limitations, that is, we can find it difficult to read the text objectively because we are too close to it. It's always a good idea to have someone else with a clear, objective eye to edit it.

DEAR WRITER

I HOPE that in the pages above, you have gained some confidence and excitement as you accompany your characters on a compelling journey through this stage of their lives, that you can place them in rich settings enhanced by your use of figurative language, and that some of those sticky grammar issues are remedied and are now well-oiled tools in your writing box.

Remember, that whether you want to be read or not, keeping a reader in mind will help you to refine your writing so that the beautiful images, the poignant moments are transferred seamlessly from your mind into another's.

Writing is a wonderful profession, vocation, and pastime, and I hope that, above all, it brings you great joy.

Good luck,

Amanda

ACKNOWLEDGMENTS

The writing of this volume, and this series, has arisen from my experiences in as a teacher and mentor of creative writing. I would like to thank all my students, past and current, who continue to inspire me, excite me, and who enrich my own writing.

My sincere thanks go to my publisher, Miika Hannila and the team at Next Chapter for their incredible support of both the work and the author.

As always, thanks to Chris for the love and the cups of tea and cake as I tap away at the keyboard.

ABOUT THE AUTHOR

Amanda Apthorpe PhD, MA, MSc, BEd

Amanda Apthorpe is a published writer and an educator who holds degrees in science, the arts and education.

Following the publication of her first novel and, after twenty-five years as a teacher of Science, Amanda took a new path to follow her dream as a writer and teacher of writing. During this time, she completed her PhD, which culminated in the publication of her second novel.

Her four novels to date, *Whispers in the Wiring*, *A Single Breath*, *Hibernia* and *One Core Belief* are published by Next Chapter.

Amanda has presented papers on creative writing at conferences in Wellington NZ and London UK, has been interviewed on radio, has convened workshops for Writers Victoria, and she is the author *Write This Way* series – Volumes 1-4 – published by Next Chapter.

Amanda teaches at Swinburne University of Technology, Victoria University, and the Centre for Adult Education, and is currently writing her fifth novel.

To learn more about Amanda Apthorpe and discover more Next Chapter authors, visit our website at www.nextchapter.pub.

Write Compelling Plots
ISBN: 978-4-82415-324-1

Published by
Next Chapter
2-5-6 SANNO
SANNO BRIDGE
143-0023 Ota-Ku, Tokyo
+818035793528

6th October 2022